The presiding minister (called
the president), at the celebration of
Holy Communion, enters and
may say one of the Seasonal Sentences,
or a hymn or psalm may be sung.

The president may say:

(2) **The Lord be with you**

All reply:

and also with you.

The following prayer may be said:

(3) **Almighty God,**
to whom all hearts are open,
all desires known,
and from whom no secrets are hidden:
cleanse the thoughts of our hearts
by the inspiration of your Holy Spirit,
that we may perfectly love you,
and worthily magnify your holy name;
through Christ our Lord. Amen.

(Prayers of Penitence may be said here or later.)

The Kyries may be said or sung, where we ask God to have mercy on us for our sins.

(Or the Gloria in Excelsis, on the opposite page, may follow.)

(9) Lord, have mercy.
Lord, have mercy.

Christ, have mercy.
Christ, have mercy.

Lord, have mercy.
Lord, have mercy.

(10) Glory to God in the highest,
and peace to his people on earth.

Lord God, heavenly King,
almighty God and Father,
we worship you, we give you thanks,
we praise you for your glory.

Lord Jesus Christ, only Son of the Father,
Lord God, Lamb of God,
you take away the sin of the world:
have mercy on us;
you are seated at the right hand of the Father:
receive our prayer.

For you alone are the Holy One,
you alone are the Lord,
you alone are the Most High,
Jesus Christ,
with the Holy Spirit,
in the glory of God the Father. Amen.

The Collect of the day comes next. This is a special prayer for each Sunday, to collect together the Church's thoughts and offer thanks to God. (see page 397 onwards in *The Alternative Service Book 1980.*)

THE MINISTRY OF THE WORD

Listen carefully to God's teaching around the theme for this Sunday.
A reading from the Old Testament may follow.

The New Testament reading for the Sunday may be read by a member of the congregation. It is usually taken from one of the letters, most of which were written by Saint Paul to the early Christians, and read out to them when they met for worship.

At the end of each reading the reader may say:

(13, 15)   ## This is the word of the Lord.

All reply:

Thanks be to God.

A hymn or psalm may be sung.

Stand for the Gospel reading. The Gospels tell us what Jesus did and said. When the Gospel for the Sunday is announced, say:

(17)   ## Glory to Christ our Saviour.

At the end of the Gospel the reader says:

This is the Gospel of Christ.

All reply:

Praise to Christ our Lord.

Sit quietly and listen to the Sermon or short talk which usually follows.

Stand to say the statement
about the Christian Faith,
called The Nicene Creed.

(19) We believe in one God,
the Father, the almighty,
maker of heaven and earth,
of all that is,
seen and unseen.

We believe in one Lord,
  Jesus Christ,
the only Son of God,
eternally begotten of the Father,
God from God, Light from Light,
true God from true God,
begotten, not made,
of one Being with the Father.
Through him all things were made.
For us men and for our salvation
he came down from heaven;
by the power of the Holy Spirit
he became incarnate of the Virgin Mary,
  and was made man.
For our sake he was crucified under
  Pontius Pilate;
he suffered death and was buried.

On the third day he rose again
in accordance with the Scriptures;
he ascended into heaven
and is seated at the right hand of the Father.
He will come again in glory
to judge the living and the dead,
and his kingdom will have no end.

We believe in the Holy Spirit,
the Lord, the giver of life,
who proceeds from the Father and the Son.
With the Father and the Son he is worshipped
    and glorified.
He has spoken through the Prophets.

We believe in one holy catholic
    and apostolic Church.
We acknowledge
    one baptism for the
    forgiveness of sins.
We look for the resurrection
    of the dead,
and the life of the world
    to come. Amen.

Now follow intercessions and short Thanksgiving prayers which may be led by a member of the congregation and may include the following:

(20, 21) Let us pray for the Church and for the world,
and let us thank God for his goodness.

Almighty God, our heavenly Father, you
promised through your Son Jesus Christ to hear
us when we pray in faith.

Strengthen . . . . . . our bishop and all your Church
in the service of Christ; that those who confess your
name may be united in your truth, live together
in your love, and reveal your glory in the world.

This response may be used with each paragraph.

Lord, in your mercy
hear our prayer.

Bless and guide Elizabeth our Queen; give
wisdom to all in authority; and direct this and
every nation in the ways of justice and of peace;
that men may honour one another, and seek the
common good.

Give grace to us, our families and friends, and to
all our neighbours; that we may serve Christ in
one another, and love as he loves us.

Comfort and heal all those who suffer in body,
mind, or spirit . . .; give them courage and hope
in their troubles; and bring them the joy of your
salvation.

Hear us as we remember those who have died in the faith of Christ . . .; according to your promises, grant us with them a share in your eternal kingdom.

Rejoicing in the fellowship of (*N* and of) all your saints, we commend ourselves and all Christian people to your unfailing love.

Merciful Father,

**accept these prayers
for the sake of your Son,
our Saviour Jesus Christ. Amen.**

The Commandments, or the following Summary of the Law, may be said.

(24) Our Lord Jesus Christ said: The first commandment is this: 'Hear, O Israel, the Lord our God is the only Lord. You shall love the Lord your God with all your heart, with all your soul, with all your mind, and with all your strength.' The second is this: 'Love your neighbour as yourself.' There is no other commandment greater than these.

Amen. Lord, have mercy.

The president may say:

(25) God so loved the world that he gave his only Son Jesus Christ to save us from our sins, to be our advocate in heaven, and to bring us to eternal life.

(26) Let us confess our sins, in penitence and faith,
firmly resolved to keep God's commandments
and to live in love and peace with all men.

(27) **Almighty God, our heavenly Father,**
we have sinned against you and against our
    fellow men,
in thought and word and deed,
through negligence, through weakness,
through our own deliberate fault.

We are truly sorry,
and repent of all our sins.
For the sake of your Son Jesus Christ, who
    died for us,
forgive us all that is past;
and grant that we may serve you in newness
    of life
to the glory of your name. Amen.

(28) Almighty God,
who forgives all who truly repent,
have mercy upon *you*,
pardon and deliver *you* from all *your* sins,
confirm and strengthen *you* in all goodness,
and keep *you* in life eternal;
through Jesus Christ our Lord. **Amen.**

(29) The following prayer may be said together.

We do not presume
to come to this your table,
    merciful Lord,
trusting in our own righteousness,
but in your manifold and great mercies.
We are not worthy
so much as to gather up the crumbs
    under your table.
But you are the same Lord
whose nature is always to have mercy.
Grant us therefore, gracious Lord,
so to eat the flesh of your dear son
    Jesus Christ
and to drink his blood,
that we may evermore dwell in him
and he in us. Amen.

THE MINISTRY OF THE SACRAMENT

(30) Stand for the Peace. The following may be said.

We are the Body of Christ.
In the one Spirit we were all baptized into
   one body.
Let us then pursue all that makes for peace
and builds up our common life.

The president then says:

The peace of the Lord be always with you

All reply:

and also with you.

A hymn may be sung, the offerings of the people may be collected and presented and the bread and wine are brought to the holy table.

(34) **Yours, Lord, is the greatness, the power,
the glory, the splendour, and the majesty;
for everything in heaven and on earth is yours.
All things come from you,
and of your own do we give you.**

(38)   The Lord is here.
His Spirit is with us.

Lift up your hearts.
We lift them to the Lord.

Let us give thanks to the Lord our God.
It is right to give him thanks and praise.

It is indeed right,
it is our duty and our joy,
at all times and in all places
to give you thanks and praise,
holy Father, heavenly King,
almighty and eternal God,
through Jesus Christ your only Son our Lord.

For he is your living Word;
through him you have created all things from
    the beginning,
and formed us in your own image.

Through him you have freed us from the
    slavery of sin,
giving him to be born as man and to die upon
    the cross;
you raised him from the dead
and exalted him to your right hand on high.

Through him you have sent upon us
your holy and life-giving Spirit,
and made us a people for your own possession.

Therefore with angels and archangels,
and with all the company of heaven,
we proclaim your great and glorious name,
for ever praising you and saying:

**Holy, holy, holy Lord,
God of power and might,
heaven and earth are full of your glory.
Hosanna in the highest.**

The following short Anthem may also be used.

**Blessed is he who comes in the name of
   the Lord.
Hosanna in the highest.**

Accept our praises, heavenly Father,
through your Son our Saviour Jesus Christ;
and as we follow his example and obey
   his command,
grant that by the power of your Holy Spirit
these gifts of bread and wine
may be to us his body and his blood;

Who in the same night that he was betrayed,
took bread and gave you thanks;
he broke it and gave it to his disciples,
   saying,
Take, eat; this is my body which is given
   for you;
do this in remembrance of me.
In the same way, after supper
he took the cup and gave you thanks;
he gave it to them, saying,
Drink this, all of you;
this is my blood of the new covenant,
which is shed for you and for many for the
   forgiveness of sins.

Do this, as often as you drink it,
in remembrance of me.

All say or sing:

Christ has died:
Christ is risen:
Christ will come again.

The president says:

Therefore, heavenly Father,
we remember his offering of himself
made once for all upon the cross,
and proclaim his mighty resurrection and
    glorious ascension.
As we look for his coming in glory,
we celebrate with this bread and this cup
his one perfect sacrifice.

Accept through him, our great high priest,
this our sacrifice of thanks and praise;
and as we eat and drink these holy gifts
in the presence of your divine majesty,
renew us by your Spirit,
inspire us with your love,
and unite us in the body of your Son,
Jesus Christ our Lord.

Through him, and with him, and in him,
by the power of the Holy Spirit,
with all who stand before you in earth
    and heaven,
we worship you, Father almighty,
in songs of everlasting praise:

All say or sing:

Blessing and honour and glory and power
be yours for ever and ever. Amen.

The president says:

(42) As our Saviour taught us, so we pray.

Join in saying The Lord's Prayer together

**Our Father in heaven,
hallowed be your name,
your kingdom come,
your will be done,
on earth as in heaven.
Give us today our daily bread.
Forgive us our sins
as we forgive those who sin against us.
Lead us not into temptation
but deliver us from evil.
For the kingdom, the power, and the glory
are yours
now and for ever. Amen.**

The president then breaks the bread (or wafer) and says:

(43) We break this bread
to share in the body of Christ.

All reply:

**Though we are many, we are one body,
because we all share in one bread.**

The following or another Anthem may be said or sung:

(44) **Jesus, Lamb of God: have mercy on us.
Jesus, bearer of our sins: have mercy on us.
Jesus, redeemer of the world: give us
your peace.**

(45) Draw near with faith. Receive the body of our
Lord Jesus Christ which he gave for you, and his
blood which he shed for you.

Eat and drink in remembrance that he died for
you, and feed on him in your hearts by faith with
thanksgiving.

(46) ## The body of Christ keep you in eternal life.
The blood of Christ keep you in eternal life.

The communicant replies each time:

Amen

and then receives.

During the distribution Hymns and
Anthems may be sung.

After the Communion the president may say this prayer

(52) Father of all, we give you thanks and praise, that when we were still far off you met us in your Son and brought us home. Dying and living, he declared your love, gave us grace, and opened the gate of glory. May we who share Christ's body live his risen life; we who drink his cup bring life to others; we whom the Spirit lights give light to the world. Keep us firm in the hope you have set before us, so we and all your children shall be free, and the whole earth live to praise your name; through Christ our Lord. **Amen.**

And/or this prayer may be said together.

(53) **Almighty God,
we thank you for feeding us
with the body and blood of your Son Jesus Christ.
Through him we offer you our souls and bodies
to be a living sacrifice.
Send us out
in the power of your Spirit
to live and work
to your praise and glory. Amen.**

23

A seasonal blessing, or the following,
may be said before you depart.

(54) The peace of God, which passes all
understanding, keep your hearts and minds in
the knowledge and love of God, and of his Son
Jesus Christ our Lord; and the blessing of God
almighty, the Father, the Son, and the Holy
Spirit, be among you, and remain with you
always. **Amen.**